Teaching Law Online

Teaching Law Online

Jennifer Camero

VANDEPLAS PUBLISHING, LLC
UNITED STATES OF AMERICA

Teaching law online

Camero, Jennifer

Published by:

Vandeplas Publishing, LLC – July 2015

801 International Parkway, 5th Floor
Lake Mary, FL. 32746
USA

www.vandeplaspublishing.com

ISBN 978-1-60042-264-5

For Mark

You showed me that my husband, best friend, travel companion, caregiver, and most ardent supporter can be one person.

◇◇◇◇◇◇◇◇◇◇◇◇◇◇◇◇◇◇◇◇◇◇◇◇◇◇◇◇◇◇

Table of Contents

Table of Figures

Preface

A cancer diagnosis and a spouse with a job offer he just couldn't refuse required a move from Illinois to Florida. When my law school proposed that I teach online, I jumped at the chance. I love teaching and continuing to teach rather than quit was an easy decision. Besides, how much different than teaching in a classroom could an online course be?

Unfortunately, I found out the hard way that distance education truly is different than a traditional class. While basic pedagogy may be the same, course design and instruction required a different focus and way more time and effort. As I began to design my first course, I quickly found myself overwhelmed.

Naturally, my first instinct was to research teaching law online. As I looked for books and articles, I was surprised at how little information existed on instructing online law courses. While a plethora of texts and articles exist on teaching high school and undergraduate courses online, they just didn't encompass the nuances and challenges of teaching at the law school level. Thus, after teaching ten online law courses (both substantive and skills courses), I decided to develop this concise guidebook for law professors making the jump into the online world of legal education.

This guide presumes some law school teaching experience; if this is your first time teaching any law school course, I recommend you utilize this guide in conjunction with the books listed in Appendix D. Likewise, this guide is not intended to instruct you on how to use the underlying technology (see Appendix C for a list of technological tutorials). Instead, this book is intended to guide the professor through the course design and instruction process by focusing on issues unique to distance education in the law school environment.

If you have any questions or feedback, please feel free to contact me at jcamero@siu.edu.

Acknowledgments

First, I would like to thank my husband, Mark, for his strength and unwavering support. He is my inspiration and my motivation, driving me to accomplishments I never dreamed achievable.

I also must thank the administration, faculty, staff, and students at Southern Illinois University School of Law. In particular, I am indebted to Frank Houdek who approached me about teaching via distance education and Dean Cynthia Fountaine who supported it without question. I am grateful to my mentor, Associate Dean Chris Behan, for his encouragement and friendship. Last, I thank all the students who enrolled in my online courses for their flexibility and patience.

Third, I thank the professors of the Department of Business Administration and Economics at Saint Mary's College in Notre Dame, Indiana, particularly Professor Claude Renshaw and Professor Mary Ann Merryman. They inspired me to enter the profession by modeling the ideal professor through their expertise, quality teaching, and support of every student who entered their classroom each semeser.

Additionally, I thank my parents, Nancy and George Pelic, for supporting me even when they disagreed with me, and my brother, Dr. Christopher Pelic, for setting the bar high.

Finally, I thank Vandeplas Publishing for the opportunity to share my newfound knowledge on distance education and for flexibility when cancer treatment intervened with deadlines.

Chapter 1

UNDERSTANDING THE ABA STANDARDS ON DISTANCE EDUCATION

The American Bar Association (the "ABA") is the main accreditation entity for law schools. The goal of the ABA is to ensure students receive a quality legal education. The ABA publishes Standards and Rules of Approval for Law Schools (the "ABA Standards") that each law school must meet in order to receive and retain accreditation from the ABA.

Accredited law schools complete an annual questionnaire that addresses compliance with the ABA Standards. Addtionally, the ABA reviews each accredited law school every seven years through a more detailed questionnaire and a site evaluation visit, in which approximately seven individuals visit the law school for a three-day period. The site evaluation team reviews materials supporting the completed questionnaire, meets with law school administration, faculty, and students, and attends classes to ensure continued compliance with the ABA Standards.

Recently updated, the revised ABA Standards became effective August 2014. With the exception of five specific ABA Standards that will apply beginning 2016-2017, the remaining revised ABA Standards are applicable to site visits occurring in 2015-2016.

Revised in August 2014, the ABA Standards include one section, Standard 306, which addresses distance education courses in legal education. Standard 306 defines a distance education course as "one in which students are separated from the faculty member or each other for more than one-third of the instruction and the instruction involves the use of technology to support regular and substantive interaction among students an the faculty member, either synchronously or asynchronously."

From an administrative perspective, the law school must seek approval for the distance education course through the school's curriculum approval process. The school must have the necessary faculty, staff, facilities, and technological resources to ensure a quality course. It must verify that the individual completing the course and any exams or assignments is in fact the student enrolled in the course, all while maintaining student privacy. Only students who have completed twenty-eight credit hours toward their degree may enroll in a distance education course, and they may count only fifteen credits from distance education courses toward their required degree credits.

The ABA Standards governing the structure and substance of a distance education course are relatively brief and broad.

However, you must keep them in mind when designing and teaching your online law course. In particular, you should focus on four key requirements. First, the instruction naturally must use technology such as the internet, audio conferencing, video conferencing, and any one-way or two-way communication device to deliver content and communicate with students.

Second, the course must incorporate regular and substantive interaction both among students and between the students and the professor. Because Standard 306 is relatively new, it is unclear what constitutes "substantive interaction" and how much of it is needed to be considered "regular". Based upon informal ABA documentation and ABA site evaluation team guidance, "substantive interaction" likely includes emails, discussion board posts, and synchronous discussions.

Third, the professor must regularly monitor student effort and communicate with students regarding that effort. While monitoring may include tracking student log-ins to the course website or percentage of content viewed, it also must include some sort of formative assessment, ungraded or graded (as discussed in Chapter 3).

Last, the course must have learning outcomes consistent with those outcomes listed in Standard 302, which applies to all law school courses, and include compentency in legal research, legal reasoning and analysis, substantive and procedural law, professional responsibility, and oral and written communication.

Many design and instruction recommendations included in this book are not only good practice but also necessary to meet these key requirements. Nonetheless, you should read the ABA Standards thoroughly before designing your course, specifically focusing on Standard 306. They are available to download for free from the ABA website (http://www.americanbar. org) or you can purchase a hard copy from the ABA Webstore (http://shop.americanbar.org).

Chapter 2

Choosing a Mode of Delivery

After familiarizing yourself with the ABA Standards, and in particular Standard 306, you can begin the process of developing your course. The first step to developing your course is to choose the mode of delivery, which is how you will distribute course content and interact with your students. Four methods for delivering course content of distance education courses exist - asynchronous, synchronous, hybrid, and blended - and each has its strengths and weaknesses. Careful design of your course can emphasize many of the strengths and eliminate many of the weaknesses, so allow the course, your comfort level, the school's curriculum needs, and the available technology at the school to dictate the mode of delivery.

Asynchronous

An asynchronous distance education course has no set meeting time or place. Students complete assignments when they choose subject only to any due dates you impose on them.

Students access course material via a learning management system ("LMS"), which is web-based software that houses the course content. Most law schools already have an LMS in place either through the law school itself or its affiliated university. The most popular LMSs are Blackboard, Desire2Learn ("D2L"), Moodle, and The West Education Network ("TWEN"). With the exception of TWEN, the functionality of these LMSs generally is the same. Appendix C sets forth select resources that provide detailed explanations on the features of these LMSs and tutorials on using those features.

One of the major benefits of an asynchronous course is that it provides flexibility, which is especially important to students with familial obligations, a part-time job, a clerkship, or an externship. This flexibility is often the main reason students choose to enroll in distance education courses.

Asynchronous courses also provides students practice managing time and prioritizing tasks, real workd skills that are essential to their career success. Additionally, asynchronous courses offer autonomy, which studies show leads to increased productivity and learning. This increased productivity and learning results from continual access to the material, which provides opportunity for review as well as time to deliberate before asking questions or commenting on the material.

However, because of the flexibility and autonomy, students can fall behind easily, especially underprepared students lacking basic study and time management skills. Moreover, assessing student progress requires effort as you do not have the benefit of visual clues as to student comprehension that you have in a classroom. Finally, because students access the material on their own time, little to no opportunities exist for real-time interaction and spontaneous discussions that may arise in a classroom environment.

Synchronous

In a synchronous course, students and the professor meet online at the same time for class sessions, and therefore, is most like a traditional live course. Because students and the professors meet in real-time, a synchronous course allows for more direct interaction and the use of the same pedagogy as a traditional course. As such, it is a great transition for both professors and students into distance education.

The students either can meet in one classroom with a monitor of the professor or the students can participate from any location in which they can connect to the internet. Regardless, you can conduct synchronous sessions one-way or two-way. In a one-way class, also called a closed class, students can hear (and usually see) the professor, but a student must click a button and wait for the professor to open the student's microphone in order to speak. A variety of free and paid programs exist to conduct closed classes, but the most popular are Skype, Google Hangout, Adobe Connect, and Blackboard Collaborate. In a two-way class, also called an open class, students not only can hear the professor speaking, but also can speak at will. The most popular software programs for open classes are WebEx and GoToMeeting. Appendix C provides select resources that detail the features of the programs for open and closed classes.

A main benefit to a synchronous course is that it allows for the spontaneous discussions and questions that arise in a traditional live course, discussions and questions that require more effort to replicate in an asynchronous course. However, such live interaction requires an investment in and access to technological equipment such as a video camera, microphone, and the requisite software, high speed internet access for fluid streaming, and on-call technological support to assist the professor and the students during each class session in the event of that issues arise during the session.

Hybrid

A hybrid course utilizes both synchronous and asynchronous means to deliver the course. It provides some direct interaction but is not as flexible as an asynchronous course due to some open or closed classes. For example, you can utilize a combination of one-way or two-way synchronous lectures and recorded lectures to deliver the material.

The advantages and disadvantages of a hybrid course are the same as those of an asynchronous and synchronous course depending upon the ratio of asynchronous to synchronous means utilized in the course.

Blended

A blended course, sometimes referred to as a flipped classroom, incorporates various asynchronous and synchronous delivery methods into a traditional live course. The students and faculty meet in a classroom at some regular interval, but the professor also uses technology to deliver course material. This supplementation usually takes the form of a recorded lecture in order to reserve classroom time for specific activities such as collaborative work, simulation, and problem-solving.

Depending upon the extent of asynchronous and synchronous delivery methods included in the blended course, it may not be a distance education course as defined by the ABA Standards due to the one-third requirement of Standard 306.

Chapter 3

DESIGNING THE COURSE

Designing and building an online law course requires careful thought and planning, even more so than a traditional law school course, due to the difficulty in choosing appropriate content delivery methods for the course material. Rather than merely record and post lectures, you must evaluate your course's learning objectives and outcomes conscientiously in order to choose content delivery methods that achieve those learning outcomes.

Once you have chosen your mode of delivery, you then should develop learning objectives for the course. Learning objectives are broad statements regarding the desired results of the course. In other words, learning objectives are what you want your students to know or be able to do at the end of the course.

Next, you establish learning outcomes, which are specific, measurable knowledge and skills the students possess at the end of the course. Unlike learning objectives, which are general statements on the intended results of the course, learning outcomes are express, observable results of the course. They are evidence that the students actually learned the material. For each learning objective, you should have at least one learning outcome.

Figure 3-1 provides a few examples of generic learning objectives transformed into specific learning outcomes from my Introduction to Transactional Skills course.

Figure 3-1: Sample Learning Objectives and Learning Outcomes	
Learning Objectives	**Learning Outcomes**
Understand the contract review process	Review and comment upon a contract prepared by another party
Become familiar with the content of a contract	Identify and explain the parts of a contract
Understand and perform the counseling role of a transactional attorney	Draft a letter to a client advising her on both the business and legal issues associated with a particular transaction

Once you have determined the learning objectives and related learning outcomes, you then choose the content delivery methods that best translate the objectives into outcomes. When choosing content delivery methods for a course, you need to keep in mind a number of best practices regardless of your mode of delivery:

◊ Vary content delivery methods

◊ Build a community

◊ Use technology as means, not focus

◊ Create structure

These best practices are not unique to the online learning environment; however, how you incorporate these best practices into your course design is unique.

Vary Content Delivery Methods

Research demonstrates that not all students obtain and process information in the same manner. Each student has her own learning style, and good course design takes into consideration these varied learning styles.

The most common learning styles are auditory, visual, and kinesthetic. Auditory learners learn by listening and speaking, such as listening to lectures and participating in class discussions. Visual learners, on the other hand, need some visual representation of the material, such as presentation slides, flowcharts, or diagrams. Kinesthetic learners, also called tactile learners, require some activity to learn, such as simulation or role-play.

Most students possess some combination of these learning styles rather than just one, although they likely have a dominate style. Incorporating a variety of content delivery methods in your course accommodates each of these learning styles and helps to ensure you reach the greatest number of students.

Not only does variety accomodate varying learning styles, but it also keeps students engaged and motivated, which is especially important in an asynchronous distance education course. When students are away from the law school environment, such as at home in front of a computer, it is easy for them to become distracted or allow their minds to drift. Variety alleviates boredom and creates interest, thus reducing the chance of the students diverting their attention away from the material.

With today's technology, numerous options exist for content delivery. The first, and most commonly used, delivery method is lecture. You can record or broadcast live audio or video lectures similar to your traditional classroom lectures. However, in order to maintain student engagement, a good practice is keep the lectures short (twenty minutes or less). If necessary, you can break up a long lecture into smaller lectures or use "commercials" such as a quizzes or discussions. Even if you choose an audio lecture to avoid being on camera, I strongly recommend some visual representation of the material, such as PowerPoint slides, to focus the students on the material and to reach visual learners.

Popular lecture recording software includes Panopto, Adobe Captivate, and D2L Capture, and all allow you to incorporate presentation slides either through the software itself or by linking a PowerPoint presentation. If your course is synchronous, live lecture broadcast software options include WebEx, D2L Capture, Adobe Connect, and Blackboard Collaborate, depending on whether your course is one-way or two-way as discussed in Chapter 2.

The second available content delivery method is discussion board threads. Discussion board posts and responses are effective as they give the students time to reflect on a topic or issue and draft a thoughtful and meaningful response. As such, they help develop critical thinking and writing skills, which are important in the law school setting and in the practice of law.

Discussion board posts can be directed, where you provide a topic or question you want the student to address, or open, where students can choose the subject of their posts. When utilizing directed discussion board posts, you need to carefully draft the question. You want to avoid leading questions, asking multiple questions in one thread, and questions with yes/no answers. When drafting a question for a discussion board, you should think about what skill you want the student to use and what knowledge you want the student to demonstrate. Types of discussion questions include:[1]

- Exploratory = examine basic facts and demonstrate basic knowledge
- Challenge = question assumptions or conclusions
- Relational = compare ideas, topics, or issues
- Diagnostic = examine motives
- Action = analyze an issue and reach a conclusion
- Cause-and-Effect = determine causal relationship
- Extension = expand a discussion of a previously-discussed issue
- Hypothetical = analyze an imagined scenario
- Priority = identify the key issue
- Summary = summarize knowledge

Regardless of whether you incorporate directed or open discussion board posts, you should provide sample posts and responses so students understand your expectations.

Another method of delivery content is through collaborative work. Students work together to prepare assignments or projects using email, video conference, phone, discussion boards, and document sharing. Collaborative work develops interpersonal and communication skills, introduces students to other perspectives,

---

1   Barbara Gross Davis, Tools for Teaching (Jossey-Bass 2009).

teaches project management, prepares students for the teamwork required in law practice, and creates accountability.

The biggest obstacle to a successful collaboration, however, is ensuring equal contributions by all group members. Although the students are in ultimate control of how much they contribute, you can take certain measures to incentivize participation.

First, whether you assign teams or allow the students to choose teams, keep the groups small. Smaller groups of three to five students allow for more meaningful collaboration and help minimize less involved students who would otherwise get by doing less work in a larger group.

Second, you should require each team to develop a code of conduct or team contract that includes: (i) team expectations and goals; (ii) contact information; (iii) preferred form of communication; (iv) distribution of work; (v) conflict resolution procedures; (vi) project plan; and (vii) meeting format and frequency. Codes of conduct and team contracts focus the students on key components of successful collabortion and help prevent issues that often arise with group assignments.

Third, you can create a private discussion board for each group and require communication via that board. By monitoring the discussions, you can get a sense of individual contributions and intervene if needed, as well as provide the students more individualized guidance.

Fourth, you can require the students to complete a peer evaluation of their group members as well as a self evaluation midway through the collaboration and use those evaluations to spot any issues requiring intervention. Figure 3-2 is a sample peer evaluation

Figure 3-2: Sample Peer Evaluation

Name_____

Name of Team Member Being Evaluated

_____

For each statement below, rate your team member on the following scale:

    1 = Strongly disagree
    2 = Disagree
    3 = Neither disagree or agree
    4 = Agrees
    5 = Strongly agrees

_____ Attended meetings
_____ Contributed meaningfully to discussions
_____ Completed work on time
_____ Prepared quality work product (accurate and thorough)
_____ Cooperated and supported team members
_____ Communicated effectively and respectfully
_____ Prioritized and managed tasks
_____ Listed to team members

For any statement that you ranked 1 or 2, please explain:

List the specific tasks, if any, this team member completed for the project:

General comments:

form your students can complete, and you also can adapt it to a self evaluation form.

Finally, each student's grade for the project can consist of two components: a grade for the end work product of the group and a grade for the individual student contribution as determined by both peer evaluations and self evaluations completed at the end of the project.

The fourth content delivery method is the use of student-centered learning activities. Student-centered learning, also called active learning, shifts the role of instructor from professor to student such that the professor becomes a facilitator and observer rather than a teacher. Research demonstrates that utilizing active learning empowers students and leads students to become more invested in the course. It also develops critical thinking and problem-solving skills because it requires the students to work through the material on their own.

The quintessential active learning method is the use of problems, exercises, or hypotheticals, which help students elucidate legal rules and apply those rules to a set of facts to reach a legal conclusion. You can create your own or use ones provided in your course textbook or supplement.

Likwise, simulation and role-play through drafting legal documents, counseling clients, negotiating with classmates, and various trial practice all constitute active learning by requiring students to determine the appropriate legal rules and apply them to the facts or issue at hand. They also provide students the opportunity to receive practical experience and see how their knowledge applies to law practice.

Another option is for students to create video or audio lectures on the material either individually or in groups. If utilizing student lectures, you need to ensure the complexity of the material is appropriate for the skill level of the students. You also need to provide adequate guidance on your expectations in terms of time, depth of discussion, and format. Student-led lectures seem to work best as introductions to the material, with your lecture filling gaps or correcting mistakes.

Build a Community

Your course should build a community in order to create trust and accountability both between student and professor and among students themselves. Trust and accountability promote learning as students are more comfortable speaking, collaborating, and being actively involved in the learning process.

Unlike a traditional course where community often develops organically, creating a community can be difficult in an online course where students never see their classmates or professor. You need to consciously include community-building activities into the first week and continue them throughout the course.

An icebreaker post at the beginning of the course is an easy and effective way to establish community roots. By sharing information about themselves and reading information about others, students feel part of a class rather than just another name or picture on a computer screen. One icebreaker I have found effective requires the students to post a picture or short video and explain how it represents why they enrolled in the course. Another option is to place students into small, random groups and require them to find a commonality among them using the discussion board.

Discussion board posts are also a valuable way to create community. Requiring regular posts and responses allows students to open up and learn from each other, just as they do in a traditional classroom setting. Each student has a voice and are more likely to open up online where they would not in a classroom setting.

Collaborative work likewise encourages community. Students tend to communicate more freely in smaller groups, because they feel more comfortable that their opinion matters and is respected. This comfort often translates into the course as a whole through increased participation in discussion board posts and other communications.

Use Technology As Means, Not Focus

Design your course using technology as the means, not the focus. The underlying technology should not distract students from learning nor should they waste their time dealing with technological issues. The best way to avoid technological distractions is to ensure students know how to use the technology required for the course through the use of a required technology workshop or online tutorials prior to or at the very beginning of the course. Also, if the course requires certain technological requirements, such as a particular program or hardware, be sure the students are aware of these requirements prior to the course. Finally, provide links and contact information for technological assistance in the syllabus and on the course webpage so students know who to contact in the event of issues or questions that inevitably will arise during the course.

Create Structure

Similar to a traditional class, you need to create structure by dividing the course into units of topic, time, or learning objective. Organizing the course into logical units helps make the material more manageable for students, leading to lower withdrawal rates and a better student experience. A well-structured course establishes expectations and builds time management skills. Structure is especially important in an asynchronous course, which requires more discipline and motivation that a traditional course or even synchronous course.

You also want to avoid posting all of the material at one time to prevent information overload and to focus the student on the appropriate material. I recommend releasing the material periodically (e.g. weekly or daily) or once a student completes a certain task. Most LMS allow you to create conditions such that it releases content at a predetermined time or only when a student completes specific tasks.

Figure 3-3: Course Design Summary
1. Develop Learning Objectives
2. Establish Learning Outcomes
3. Choose Content Delivery Methods
• Lectures (audio or visual)
• Discussion boards (directed or open)
• Collaborative work
• Student-centered learning activities (problems, hypotheticals, simulations, role-play, or student-led lectures)
4. Keep in Mind Best Practices
• Vary content delivery methods
• Build a community
• Use technology as means, not focus
• Create structure

Chapter 4

SETTING AND MAINTAINING THE TONE AND EXPECTATIONS

While many law students have taken an online course before, for many students, your course likely is their first online law course and they often are surprised at how different and more strenuous an online law course is from other courses. Therefore, setting the tone and expectations early in four key areas is critical to a successful distance education course for both you and your students.

Before the first day of the course, you must establish a strong faculty presence and maintain that presence throughout the course. Faculty presence shows passion for and devotion to the course, which research indicates motivates and stimulates students. Additionally, when students know you are heavily involved and invested in the course, they know they are accountable. This accountability ensures they put forth the required time and effort into the course and the assignments.

Continual communication with the students not only is crtitical to establishing your faculty presence, but also ensures you meet Standard 306's "regular and substantive interaction". Also, students learn how to communicate with others professionally by your example, thus, continuous communications between you and your students teach them valuable professional oral and written communication skills.

The discussion boards are a great way to communicate with students. In addition to posing questions for the students, you can add your own persective on the topic. Moreover, summarizing a thread after it has had time to develop allows students to synthesize that particular thread with the rest of the material. My general rule is that I create at least one response to every thread on the discussion boards. Student participation and effort tends to increase the more active I am in the discussion boards, because they know I read their responses.

Communicating with students also includes availability via email, phone, or video conference. You can establish virtual office hours when students know you will be available by one of these means, or you can have students reach out as needed. The key is that students should feel you are just as available, if not more so, than in a traditional law school course.

Second, you need to reinforce that an online course requires the same, if not more, time and effort than any other law school course. Students tend to believe that online courses are less strenuous than a traditional law school course, so you need to state explicitly and repetitively the amount of work necessary to succeed in the course.

Students also need to understand that they must actively participate in the course rather than merely watch lectures and submit assignments. They must comprehend your expectations with respect to the substance and form of assignments, as well as proper and professional communication methods.

Finally, you should communicate learning objectives and outcomes to students at the begining of the course. As discussed in Chapter 3, learning ojectives are broad statements of what you want your students to know, while learning outcomes are specific, measurable knowledge and skills the students possess at the end of the course. Conveying learning objectives and outcomes to students not only provides a roadmap of the course but also provides guidelines for assessment.

Setting the proper tone and expectations of the course, especially in the four key areas, starts with a detailed syllabus. Students tend to view the syllabus as a contract so you need to be clear, concise, and thorough. In addition to the basics of any good syllabus (e.g. course description, learning objectives and outcomes, grade components, and schedule), the syllabus of an online course must acquaint students with course logistics and the underlying technology.

In particular, the syllabus should discuss the course delivery method (i.e. synchronous, asynchronous, hybrid, or blended) and ensure students understand what that means. Related to the course delivery method, you should address the technological requirements to access the course materials. Also, create a technology outage policy that sets standards for when a technology outage prevents completion of an assignment.

Moreover, you need to include netiquette rules in the syllabus. Netiquette rules set standards of respectful, and polite communication in the course. Students, especially those students recently graduated from college, are acclimated to informal communication. Incorporating a netiquette policy teaches students professional, sensitive, and ethical communication skills as well as leads to a more positive experience by building a comfortable course community. Figure 4-1 provides a sample netiquette policy.

Because law school syllabi tend to be long, students often skim or simply not read them. In order to ensure a thorough review, I recommend creating a multiple choice quiz in the LMS on the contents of the syllabus. You can choose to make it a small portion of the grade or require completion (and perhaps answer a certain percentage of answers correctly) in order to access the rest of the course materials.

In addition to the syllabus, a course introduction video or podcast helps sets the proper tone and establish your expectations. A course introduction reinforces and further explains the course structure and policies, and better reaches visual and auditory learners. Similar to the syllabus, you may want to set release conditions in the LMS that require viewing of the introduction before the student can access the rest of materials.

Another way to establish tone and expectations is to provide sample work product, especially with respect to the discussion board posts. Samples provide students a sense of the form and substance expected of their work product.

Last, approximately a week before the course begins, send a welcome email that attaches the syllabus, directs students to the course

Figure 4-1: Sample Netiquette Policy

Netiquette refers to acting in a respectful and professional manner while interacting with your professor and classmates online. Keep the following rules in mind during this course:

- This course is more than learning facts; you are preparing for a career. You are learning to interact with your classmates as you would in your future professional life.
- Everyone is entitled to have an opinion. In discussion forums, everyone is encouraged to share them in a polite and respectful manner.
- People have the right to disagree with you. However, disagreement should never be personal.
- You should review your posts before you publish them for unintended meanings.
- Culture influences communication in terms of phrasing and word choice. Also, the lack of visual and auditory clues may affect meaning. Before jumping to conclusions, you should ask for clarification.
- You should respond honestly but thoughtfully and respectfully, using language which others will not consider foul or abusive.
- You must sign your name to any post.
- You must respect your own privacy and the privacy of others by not revealing information which you deem private or which you feel might embarrass you or others.
- You should always provide constructive responses to your classmates.

If you experience any questionable or outright inappropriate behavior from a classmate, please let me know immediately. I have the sole discretion to deduct points or remove a student from the course for conduct or communications violating these rules.

website with access information, notes any special technological requirements, and guides students to the technology tutorials, course introduction, and sample discussion posts. I also include in that email suggested books and webpages that provide tips for a successful online experience. Sending it before the course begins gives students time to understand the required commitment of a distance education course and ensures technological requirements are met prior to class starting.

Chapter **5**

ASSESSING STUDENTS

Assessment is the evaluation of student learning and is either summative or formative. Summative assessment occurs at the end of a topic or at the end of the course, and usually accounts for a majority, if not all, of the students' grades. The purpose of summative assessment is to determine whether students actually achieved the learning outcomes of the course by comparing each student's work product to a rubric as well as the other students' work product.

Formative assessment, on the other hand, occurs throughout the semester. Students take quizzes, write essays or memos, answer problems, complete exercises, or role play, and then receive feedback on the work product. The prompt feedback should state why the student is correct or specifically explain what the student needs to improve and how to do so. The feedback also should reflect the student's progress toward the learning outcomes and identify each student's strengths and weaknesses.

Most law courses only contain summative assessment in the form of an exam, paper, or project at the end of the course. However, formative assessment is crucial to student success in any law course, especially a distance learning course, because it evaluates student progress toward the course's learning outcomes and provides the student an opportunity to utilize that feedback to adjust study methods or focus on a particular topic or skill during the course. Additionally, formative assessment ensures compliance with ABA Standard 306, which requires "regular and substantive interaction between faculty member and student" and "regular monitoring of student effort... and...communication about that effort." Finally, formative assessment helps keep students honest by requiring them to stay on top of the readings, lectures, and assignments.

Your course structure should dictate when you incorporate formative assessment. As discussed in Chapter 3, you should divide your course into units of topic, time, or learning objective. At the completion of each unit, have your students complete an assignment, graded or ungraded, in which you provide prompt feedback so both you and the students can assess their mastery of that particular unit.

Many professors shy away from formative assessment due to the time it takes to provide individual feedback to each student. Although individual feedback by the professor is ideal, it is not the only way to provide prompt and meaningful feedback to students during the course.

You can utilize rubrics, which set forth criteria that are scored by rank or points. A rubric identifies components of the assignment, such as substance, writing competency, or citation form. Within each component, the rubric describes attributes of the component then provides a rank or point system that indicates the level of mastery of that attribute. The attributes focus students on the critical aspects of the assginment while the ranking or point system allows students to identify their strengths and weaknesses. If you are unfamiliar with rubrics, Appendix E lists resources to assist drafting rubrics in the law school setting.

Using a rubric rather than providing individualized feedback allows you to streamline the grading process while still providing formative assessment to the students. Alternatively, you can distribute the rubric after the assignment is due and require self-evlauation, peer-evaluation, or both, which is particularly useful in larger courses. If you do choose to use self-evaluation or peer-evluation, you should require the students to submit the completed rubric to you to ensure the level of quality and effort. Also, at least for the initial self- or peer-evaluation, provide feedback on the completed rubric or examples of both effective and ineffective completed rubrics so students learn how to provide constructive feedback to others and to themselves. Finally, I recommend using anonymous peer evaluation for more thorough and objective feedback.

Another substitute for individualized feedback is the distribution of a model or sample work product to which the students can compare their work product. Note that the use of a model or sample is only effective as formative assessment if it is clear to the students why the model or sample is good or bad. Therefore, you should provide comments on the model or sample answer.

Alternatively, you can create a discussion board and ask questions that focus the students on the strengths and weaknesses of the sample or model answer.

Regardless of the type of assessment, a major concern in a distance education course is cheating and plagiarism. Local test centers, remote proctoring, virtual proctoring, and plagiarism detection software help deter and discover cheating and plagiarism in distance education courses. They also help the law school satisfy ABA Standard 306(g) and Interpretation 306-2 by confirming that the exam taker is the student enrolled in the course.

Test centers provide live, proctored exams to students enrolled in online courses. Students generally are responsible for locating a certified proctor near their location, scheduling the exam, and paying any fee. You approve of the proctor and provide the exam and instructions directly to the proctor.

With remote proctoring, a proctor observes each student take the exam online using a webcam and microphone to ensure the student does not cheat. Remote proctor services are coupled with software that locks down the student's computer in order to duplicate the environment of a live, proctored exam.

Virtual proctoring utilizes a webcam and microphone to record each student during the exam. Some providers use software to spot unusual activity, such as eye movement away from the computer screen, multiple voices, or movement in the room, then spot audit exams. Other providers have certified proctors review each exam session afterwards to ensure authenticity.

Plagiarism detection software compares student submissions to other submissions in the class, to submission of students from previous classes in which you used the software, and to work product found online. The software then creates a report that indicates the originality of the work product, which assists you in determining whether the submission requires further investigation for plagiarism.

Appendix F provides websites to locate test centers as well as lists remote proctors, virtual proctors, and plagiarism detection software providers.

Chapter 6

DISTANCE EDUCATION AND THE TENURE-TRACK PROFESSOR

Distance education often is stigmatized in the law school setting. Many professors view online law courses as less rigorous than traditional courses for both the students and the professor. They inaccurately view the preparation for and instruction of a distance education course as easier and less time consuming. As a result, tenure-track law professors must tread the promotion and tenure process carefully if they choose to teach a distance education course.

As part of the promotion and tenure rules, most schools require a certain course load each semester usually set by the number of course credits taught. Before agreeing to teach an online law course, you should ensure that the course counts towards those course load requirements. Many law schools' promotion and tenure rules are vague or fail to address distance education courses, so you may need to receive clarification from the dean or the chair of the promotion and tenure committee.

Even if your law school counts distance education courses toward your course load requirement, you still must demonstrate to the faculty (especially those faculty members who will vote on your promotion and tenure) the amount of work and dedication required to design and instruct an online law course. Many of my colleagues simply did not realize the effort until either they taught an online law course themselves or they had the opportunity to see my course.

Your peer teaching reviews that are part of the promotion and tenure process are one way to demonstrate the substantial workload of a distance education course. However, with very few tenured law professors teaching distance education courses, your peer evaluators likely have not encountered an online law course before and the resulting evaluation may not reflect the work and the effectiveness of the course. If your evaluator has little or no experience, I recommend offering a tour of your course and the course website. Be sure to focus on formative assessment and communications with students to indicate the regular interaction and feedback required of a successful online law course.

While the promotion and tenure committee and voting faculty members review the peer teaching evaluations, I also recommend asking for informal peer reviews from faculty members who you believer are most skeptical of online law courses. Granting them access to your course and providing a course tour are great ways not only to win over a skeptic but also to receive valuable feedback on your course.

Another way to demonstrate the effort required to design and instruct an online law course is to offer workshops for your faculty. These workshops can cover any topic on which you feel comfortable, such as best practices, design tips, or technological guidance. The key is to use your online course as an example so that faculty gain a sense of the quality of the course and the continued effort involved in teaching an online law course.

Faculty make promotion and tenure decisions by focusing on three key areas of your work: teaching, scholarship, and service. Even at law schools that view scholarship as more important than teaching effectiveness, you must balance your time effectively and efficiently to ensure excellence in all three areas. Both the development of a new distance education course and the instruction of an established distance education course requires a great deal of time, arguably more time than a traditional law school course. Thus, as a tenure-track professor, you should consider teaching only one or two distance education courses per academic year in order to provide yourself time for scholarship and service duties.

One final consideration is the lack of mentoring available to you on distance education. Although many law schools offer online courses, very few tenured or tenure-track professors teach them given their marginal status. The adjunct professors teaching the online courses are excellent resources for designing and instructing the course but are unable to offer insight on the impact on tenure or balancing workload among teaching, scholarship, and service.

If you do not have a tenured or tenure-track faculty member that can mentor you with respect to distance education, I recommend joining the Working Group for Distance Learning in Legal Education.

It is an informal association of educators working toward increased, quality distance education opportunities in the law school setting. The association meets three times a year to discuss distance education and to develop best practices, and those meetings are a wonderful opportunity to meet both tenured and tenured-track professors diving into distance legal education. You can learn more about the Working Group for Distance Learning in Legal education at www. wgdlle.org.

As a tenure-track professor, you do not need to avoid distance education courses. Instead, at most law schools, you just need to navigate the promotion and tenure process more strategically in order to showcase your hardwork and manage your time more wisely among teaching, scholarship, and service.

Appendices

Appendix A

Additional Resources on Distance Learning in Legal Education

William H. Byrnes IV, *Alternative Methods of Teaching and the Effectiveness of Teaching and the Effectiveness of Distance Learning for Legal Education*, available at http://ssrn.com/abstract=2487679.

Noam Ebner, Lorianne Mitchell, Jennifer Parlamis & Roy Lewicki, *Teaching Negotiation Online Part 2: Getting Started*, 29 SIGNAL, no. 1, 2014 at 12.

Linda C. Fentiman, *A Distance Education Primer: Lessons from My Life as a Dot.Edu Entrepreneur*, 6 N.C. J. LAW & TECH. 41 (2004).

David C. Matz & Noam Ebner, *Using Role-Play in Online Negotiation Teaching*, in VENTURING BEYOND THE CLASSROOM: RETHINGING NEGOTIATION TEACHING, 294 (Dri Press 2010).

Lorianne Mitchell, Jennifer Parlamis, Roy Lewicki & Noam Ebner, *Teaching Negotiation Online Part 1: Challenges and Opportunities*, 28 SIGNAL, no. 3, 2014, at 20.

Sean F. Nolon, *Using Distance Education to Teaching Environmental Problem Solving Skills and Theory*, available at http://ssrn.com/abstract=2405605.

Ellen S. Podgor, *Teaching a Live Synchronous Distance Learning Course: A Student-Focused Approach*, 2006 J. OF LAW, TECH. & POL'Y 263 (2006).

Joseph A. Rosenberg, *Confronting Cliches in Online Instruction: Using a Hybrid Model to Teach Lawyering Skills*, 12 SMU Sci. & Tech. L. Rev.19 (2008).

David I.C. Thomson, *Effective Methods for Teaching Legal Writing Online*, U. Denver Legal Studies Research Paper No. 08-17, available at http://ssrn.com/abstract=1159467.

Working Group for Distance Learning in Legal Education –www.wgdlle.org

APPENDIX B

Select Resources on Distance Education

Publications

Rita-Marie Conrad & J. Ana Donaldson, ENGAGING THE ONLINE LEARNER: ACTIVITIES AND RESOURCES FOR CREATIVE INSTRUCTION (Jossey-Bass 2011).

Sarah Cornelius, Carole Gordon & Jan Schyma, LIVE ONLINE LEARNING: STRATEGIES FOR THE WEB CONFERENCING CLASSROOM (Palgrave Macmillian 2014).

DISTANCE EDUCATION: NEW PERSPECTIVES (Keith Harry, Magnus John & Desmond Keegan, eds., Routledge 2014).

Elliot King & Neil Alperstein, BEST PRACTICES IN ONLINE PROGRAM DEVELOPMENT: TEACHING AND LEARNING IN HIGHER EDUCATION (Routledge 2014).

Susan Ko & Steve Rossen, TEACHING ONLINE: A PRACTICAL GUIDE (Routledge 2014).

Michelle Pancansky-Brock, BEST PRACTICES FOR TEACHING WITH EMERGING TECHNOLOGIES (Routledge 2013).

Robin M. Smith, CONQUERING THE CONTENT: A BLUEPRINT FOR ONLINE COURSE DESIGN AND DEVELOPMENT (Jossey-Bass 2014).

Jared Stein & Charles R. Graham, ESSENTIALS OF BLENDED TEACHING: A STANDARDS-BASED GUIDE (Routledge 2014).

Thomas J. Tobin, B. Jean Mandernach & Ann H. Taylor, EVALUATING ONLINE TEACHING: IMPLEMENTING BEST PRACTICES (Jossey-Bass 2015).

Marjorie Vai & Kristen Sosulski, ESSENTIALS OF ONLINE COURSE DESIGN:

A STANDARDS-BASED GUIDE (Routledge 2011).

Online Resources
Online Journal of Distance Learning Administration
http://www.westga.edu/~distance/ojdla/

Online Learning Consortium (formerly The Sloan Consortium)
http://onlinelearningconsortium.org

Online Learning (formerly the Journal of Asynchronous Learning Networks)
http://onlinelearningconsortium.org/publications/olj_main

The International Review of Research in Open and Distance Learning
www.irrodl.org/index.php/irrodl/index

APPENDIX C

Select Resources on Technology and Media in Distance Education

General Resources

Tony Bates, THE ROLE OF TECHNOLOGY IN DISTANCE EDUCATION (Routledge 2014).

Joanne Kaattari & Vicki Trottier, GUIDE TO TECHNOLOGIES FOR ONLINE LEARNING (Community Literacy of Ontario 2012).

Yefim Kats, LEARNING MANAGEMENT SYSTEM TECHNOLOGIES AND SOFTWARE SOLUTIONS FOR ONLINE TEACHING: TOOLS AND APPLICATIONS (Information Science Reference 2010).

Benjamin A. Perez & Timothy J. Perez, CHOOSING THE RIGHT LEARNING MANAGEMENT SYSTEM (CreateSpace Independent Publishing Platform 2011).

Adobe Captivate

Diane Elkins, Desiree Pinder & Tim Slade, E-LEARNING UNCOVERED: ADOBE CAPTIVATE 8 (CreateSpace Independent Publishing Platform 2014).

Kevin Siegel, ADOBE CAPTIVATE 8: THE ESSENTIALS (IconLogic, Inc. 2014)

Adobe Connect

www.adobe.com/products/adobeconnect.html

Milos Vucetic and Milos Radovanovic, LEARNING ADOBE CONNECT 9 (Packt Publishing 2013).

Blackboard LMS

Howie Southworth, Kemal Cakici, Yianna Vovides & Susan Zvacek,

BLACKBOARD FOR DUMMIES (For Dummies 2006).

William Rice, BLACKBOARD ESSENTIALS FOR TEACHERS (Packt Publishing 2012).

Blackboard Collaborate
www.blackboard.com/Platforms/Collaborate/Overview.aspx

Cisco WebEx
www.webex.com

Nancy Stevenson, WEBEX WEB MEETINGS FOR DUMMIES (For Dummies 2005).

Desire2Learn
Brandon Ballentine, DESIRE2LEARN FOR HIGHER EDUCATION COOKBOOK (Packt Publishing 2012).

D2L Self Directed Training, https://training.desire2learn.com/

Google Hangout
https://plus.google.com/hangouts

William Kerr, GOOGLE HANGOUT: THE ULTIMATE GUIDE TO GOOGLE HANGOUT (Amazon Digital Services, Inc. 2014).

Paul Perez, YOUR GUIDE TO LIVE PODCASTING WITH GOOGLE+ HANGOUTS ON AIR (Amazon Digital Services, Inc. 2014).

GoTo Meeting
www.gotomeeting.com

Moodle

Radana Dvorak, MOODLE FOR DUMMIES (For Dummies 2011).

Jason Hollowell, MOODLE AS A CURRICULUM AND INFORMATION MANAGEMENT SYSTEM (Packt Publishing 2011).

Susan Smith Nash & Michelle Moore, MOODLE COURSE DESIGN BEST PRACTICES (Packt Publishing 2014).

William Rice, MOODLE 2.6 ELEARNING COURSE DEVELOPMENT (Packt Publishing 2014).
William Rice, MOODLE TEACHING TECHNIQUES: CREATIVE WAYS TO USE MOODLE FOR CONSTRUCTING ONLINE LEARNING SOLUTIONS (Packt Publishing 2007).

Panopto

Panopto Tutorials, http://support.panopto.com/videos

Skype

www.skype.com

James Courtney, EXPERIENCE SKYPE TO THE MAX: THE ESSENTIAL GUIDE TO THE WORLD'S LEADING INTERNET COMMUNICATIONS PLATFORM (Apress 2015).

APPENDIX D

Select Resources on Teaching Law

Steven Friedland & Gerald Hess, TEACHING THE LAW SCHOOL CURRICULUM (Carolina Academic Press 2004).

Gerald F. Hess & Steven Friedland, TECHNIQUES FOR TEACHING LAW (Carolina Academic Press 1999).

Howard E. Katz & Kevin Francis O'Neill, STRATEGIES AND TECHNIQUES OF LAW SCHOOL TEACHING: A PRIMER FOR NEW (AND NOT SO NEW) PROFESSORS (Aspen Publishers 2009).

Madeleine Schachter, THE LAW PROFESSOR'S HANDBOOK: A PRACTICAL GUIDE TO TEACHING LAW (Carolina Academic Press 2004).

Michael Hunter Schwartz, Sophie Sparrow & Gerald Hess, TEACHING LAW BY DESIGN: ENGAGING STUDENTS FROM THE SYLLABUS TO THE FINAL EXAM (Carolina Academic Press 2009).

Michael Hunter Schwartz, Gerald Hess & Sophie M. Sparrow, WHAT THE BEST LAW TEACHERS DO (Harvard University Press 2013).

APPENDIX E

Select Resources on Rubrics

Institute for Law Teaching, www.lawteaching.org/teaching/assessment/rubrics/

Beverly Peterson Jennison, *Saving the Law Professor: Using Rubrics in the Teaching of Legal Writing to Assist in Grading Writing Assignments by Section and Provide More Effective Assessment in Less Time*, 80 UMKC L. REV. 353 (2011).

Legal Writing Institute, www.lwionline.org/grading_rubrics.html

Sandra L. Simpson, *Riding the Carousel: Making Assessment a Learning Loop through the Continuous Use of Grading Rubrics*, 6 CAN. LEGAL EDUC. ANN. REV. 35 (2011).

Sophie Sparrow, *Describing the Ball: Improve Teaching by Using Rubrics-Explicit Grading Criteria*, 2004 MICH. ST. L. REV. 1 (2004).

APPENDIX F

Select Resources on Exam Proctoring and Plagiarism Detection Software

Local Proctoring
National College Testing Association, www.ncta-testing.org

Kryterion Testing Centers, www.kryteriononline.com

Remote and Virtual Proctoring
B Virtual Inc., http://bvirtualinc.com/

Proctor Free, http://proctorfree.com/

ProctorU, www.proctoru.com

Remote Proctor, www.softwaresecure.com

VProctor, www.vproctor.com

Webassessor, www.kryteriononline.com

Plagiarim Detection Software
SafeAssign, www.lexisnexis.com/documents/
LawSchoolTutorials/20091102103551_small.pdf

Turnitin, www.turnitin.com

Index